Soccer in South America

By
Mike Kennedy

with Mark Stewart

NORWOODHOUSE PRESS

Norwood House Press, P.O. Box 316598, Chicago, Illinois 60631

For information regarding Norwood House Press,
please visit our website at: www.norwoodhousepress.com or call 866-565-2900.

Photo Credits:
   All interior photos provided by Getty Images.
Cover Photos:
   Top Left: Sports Illustrated for Kids/TIME Inc.
   Top Right: Getty Images.
   Bottom Left: David Cannon/Getty Images.
   Bottom Right: Futera FZ LLC.
The soccer memorabilia photographed for this book is part of the authors' collections:
   Page 10) Kaka: Futera FZ LLC.
   Page 12) Labruna: Hotspur Boys' Paper; Pele: Panini; Maradona: Match! Magazine;
      Francescoli: Match! Magazine.
   Page 13) Ronaldo: World Soccer Magazine/IPC Media Ltd; Ronaldinho: Topps Trading Cards;
      Marta: Sports Illustrated for Kids/TIME Inc.; Messi: Futera FZ LLC.

Designer: Ron Jaffe
Project Management: Black Book Partners, LLC
Editorial Production: Jessica McCulloch
Special thanks to Ben and Bill Gould

Library of Congress Cataloging-in-Publication Data
   Kennedy, Mike, 1965-
   Soccer in South America / by Mike Kennedy, with Mark Stewart.
      p. cm. -- (Smart about sports)
   Includes bibliographical references and index.
   Summary: "An introductory look at the soccer teams and their fans of
countries in South America. Includes a brief history, facts, photos,
records, and glossary"--Provided by publisher.
   ISBN-13: 978-1-59953-446-6 (library ed. : alk. paper)
   ISBN-10: 1-59953-446-0 (library ed. : alk. paper)
   1. Soccer--South America--Juvenile literature. 2. Soccer teams--South
America--Juvenile literature. I. Stewart, Mark, 1960- II. Title.
   GV944.S63K46 2011
   796.334098--dc22
                                          2010044555

Manufactured in the United States of America in North Mankato, Minnesota.
170N–012011

Contents

Words in **bold type** are defined on page 24.

Players from Chile hug each other after a win.

4

Where in the World?

South America is home to 13 countries and more than 350 million people. They love soccer. The best South American players and teams are known all over the world.

Once Upon a Time

Soccer came to South America from Europe in the 1800s. In 1930, Uruguay held the first **World Cup**. Today, it is the biggest sports tournament on the planet. Uruguay, Brazil, and Argentina have all won the World Cup.

The great Pele
helped Brazil win
three World Cups.

7

Futuro palco da final da Copa de 2014.

MARACA. *Que bonito é.*

Players and young fans walk on the field at Maracana Stadium.

IPATINGA

At the Stadium

Brazil's Maracana Stadium is one of the best places to watch soccer. It was built for the World Cup in 1950. Brazilian fans cheer loudest when a team scores using skill and teamwork.

Town & Country

Ricardo Kaka played for a **club** in Spain in 2010. He also played for the **national team** of his home country of Brazil. Many South American soccer stars wear two uniforms during the same season.

Ricardo Kaka wears the uniform of his Spanish club.

Shoe Box

The soccer collection on these pages belongs to the authors. It shows some of the top South American stars.

Angel Labruna

ANGEL LABRUNA

Striker • Argentina
Angel Labruna was the star of a high-scoring team called "The Machine."

Pele

BRASIL

PELÉ 1970

Midfielder • Brazil
Most people think Pele was the best player ever. He scored more than 1,000 goals.

Diego Maradona

MATCH WORLD CUP WONDERS

No. 9 Diego Maradona (Argentina)

Forward • Argentina
Diego Maradona was almost unstoppable when he had the ball.

Enzo Francescoli

MATCH WORLD CUP WONDERS

No. 25 Enzo Francescoli (Uruguay)

Midfielder • Uruguay
Enzo Francescoli was a smooth shooter and passer.

World Cup Superstars
RONALDO
Brazil and Internazionale

WORLD
SOCCER

Ronaldo

Striker • Brazil
Ronaldo was
soccer's best scorer
during the 1990s.

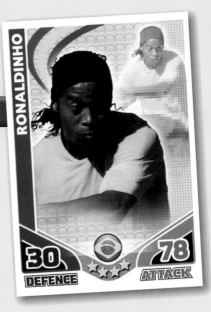

RONALDINHO

30
DEFENCE

78
ATTACK

Ronaldinho

Forward • Brazil
Ronaldinho
reminded fans of
Ronaldo. His
name means
"little Ronaldo."

MARTA
Forward • Los Angeles Sol

Marta

Forward • Brazil
Marta was named
Player of the Year
from 2006 to 2009.

STRIKER

Messi

Lionel Messi

Forward • Argentina
Lionel Messi showed
that small players
could score big goals.

13

Can't Touch This

Goalkeepers are the only players in soccer that can touch the ball with their hands. Their job is to stop goals. Sometimes goalkeepers have to leap through the air to make a "save."

David Ospina of Colombia jumps high to make a save.

Gabriela Chavez of Argentina "heads" the ball.

Just For Kicks

Watching soccer is more fun when you know some of the rules:

- You cannot touch the ball with your arms or hands.

- You can use your head to pass or shoot the ball.

- You cannot push other players.

- You can protect yourself with your arms.

On the Map

Every country in South America has its own soccer **league**.

1. Argentina
2. Bolivia
3. Brazil
4. Chile
5. Colombia
6. Ecuador
7. French Guiana
8. Guyana
9. Paraguay
10. Peru
11. Suriname
12. Uruguay
13. Venezuela

CORREO·DEL·PARAGUAY·
CAMPEONATO·MUNDIAL·DE·FUTBOL·
COPA·JULES·RIMET·CHILE·1962·
0.30 ₲

9 Paraguay

Guyana
1989

8 Guyana

R.O. del URUGUAY CORREOS
7 CTS.
IV CAMPEONATO MUNDIAL DE FUTBOL

12 Uruguay

Many countries have their own soccer stamps!

Stop Action

The goalkeeper makes a save.

Goalkeepers wear padded gloves.

Brazil's Cristiane tries to score a goal.

All players wear shin guards.

We Won!

South America has some of the best teams in the world!

Men's Soccer	World Cup Champion	Olympic* Champion
Uruguay	1930 & 1950	1924 & 1928
Argentina	1978 & 1986	2004 & 2008
Brazil	1958, 1962, 1970, 1994, & 2002	

Women's Soccer	World Cup Runner-Up	Olympic* Runner-Up
Brazil	2007	2004 & 2008

The Olympics are a worldwide sports competition. Soccer has been part of the Olympics since 1900.

Happy Brazilian players hold the World Cup trophy in 2002.

Soccer Words

CLUB
Another word for team.

LEAGUE
A group of teams that competes against each other.

NATIONAL TEAM
A team made up of players from the same country.

WORLD CUP
The tournament that decides the world champion of soccer. The World Cup is played every four years.

Index

Photos are on **bold** numbered pages.

Learn More

Learn more about the World Cup at www.fifa.com

Learn more about men's soccer at www.mlssoccer.com

Learn more about women's soccer at www.womensprosoccer.com